# IDENTIFYING CRITICAL CONTENT

## CLASSROOM TECHNIQUES TO HELP STUDENTS KNOW WHAT IS IMPORTANT

# IDENTIFYING CRITICAL CONTENT

## CLASSROOM TECHNIQUES TO HELP STUDENTS KNOW WHAT IS IMPORTANT

Deana Senn, Amber C. Rutherford,
and Robert J. Marzano

1400 Centrepark Blvd, Suite 1000
West Palm Beach, FL 33401
717-845-6300

email: pub@learningsciences.com
learningsciences.com

Printed in the United States of America

20  19  18  17  16  15          2  3  4

FSC
www.fsc.org
MIX
Paper from
responsible sources
FSC® C112431

Library of Congress Control Number: 2014939918

ISBN: 978-1-941112-00-7

# Dedication

*"If I have seen further, it is by standing on the shoulders of giants."* —Sir Isaac Newton

*I dedicate this work to my current and former colleagues in the U.S. and Alberta.*

—Deana Senn

*I dedicate this work to improving education for all learners worldwide, including my sons Brayden, Jackson, and Landon.*

—Amber C. Rutherford

# Acknowledgments

Learning Sciences International would like to thank the following reviewers:

Gay F. Barnes
Horizon Elementary School
Madison, Alabama

David Bosso
2012 Connecticut Teacher of the Year
Berlin High School
Berlin, Connecticut

Cathy Cartier
English Teacher, ELA Curriculum
   Co-chair
Affton High School
St. Louis, Missouri

Mary Eldredge-Sandbo
Biology Teacher
Des Lacs-Burlington High School
Des Lacs, North Dakota

Michael R. Fryda
Science Teacher
Westside High School
Omaha, Nebraska

Angelica Jordan
2011 State Teacher of the Year
Instructional Coach for Mathematics
Stuttgart, Germany

Daniele Massey
2013 Teacher of the Year
Department of Defense Education
   Activity

Kristen Merrell
Kindergarten Teacher
Lee's Summit Elementary School
Lee's Summit, Missouri

Karen Morman
Instructional Coach
J. W. Webb Elementary School
McKinney, Texas

Angela D. Mosier
Math Department Head,
   2013 Nebraska Teacher of the Year
Westside High School
Omaha, Nebraska

Tiffany Richard
Biology & Chemistry Teacher,
   2012 Kansas Teacher of the Year
Olathe East High School
Olathe, Kansas

Leigh M. VandenAkker
2012 Utah Teacher of the Year
East High School
Salt Lake City, Utah

Jessica Waters
2013 Rhode Island Teacher of the Year
Rhode Island

Brenda Werner
Associate Professor, Education Chair
University of Mary
Bismarck, North Dakota

Natalie Wester
2nd Grade Teacher
Gearity Professional Development
  School
University Heights, Ohio

Maryann Woods-Murphy
2010 New Jersey Teacher of the Year
Teaneck, New Jersey

# Table of Contents

# About the Authors

**DEANA SENN, MSSE,** is an expert in instructional strategies and classroom assessments. She is the Lead Content Developer and a Senior Staff Developer for Learning Sciences Marzano Center. Ms. Senn's curriculum, instruction, and assessment experience spans the United States and Canada. Ms. Senn has been a teacher and leader in school, district, regional, and provincial roles in both rural and urban settings. She is a graduate of Texas A&M University and received her master's degree from Montana State University. With her extensive experience focusing on teaching and learning, Ms. Senn offers a unique perspective for improving instructional practice.

**AMBER C. RUTHERFORD, MSEd,** works closely with Dr. Robert J. Marzano in designing content for professional development for an international audience with a particular focus on Common Core State Standards and teacher evaluation. She is a notable speaker and leads professional development throughout the nation in districts that are implementing Marzano evaluation models. Ms. Rutherford received her Master of Science in Education from Fitchburg State College and has been a successful teacher, coach, public school administrator, and certified observer in the Marzano models. As a PLC consultant, she developed PLC implementation plans that significantly raised student achievement. Her experience and commitment as a practitioner and leader in public schools guides her research in educator development for diverse populations. Amber is married to her college sweetheart, Jared, and has three rambunctious boys under the age of 5: Brayden, Jackson, and Landon.

 **ROBERT J. MARZANO** is CEO of Marzano Research Laboratory and executive director of the Learning Sciences Marzano Center for Teacher and Leader Evaluation. A leading researcher in education, he is a speaker, trainer, and author of more than 150 articles on topics such as instruction, assessment, writing and implementing standards, cognition, effective leadership, and school intervention. He has authored over 30 books, including *The Art and Science of Teaching* (ASCD, 2007) and *Teacher Evaluation That Makes a Difference* (ASCD, 2013).

# Introduction

This guide, *Identifying Critical Content: Classroom Techniques to Help Students Know What Is Important*, is intended as a resource for improving a specific element of instructional practice—*identifying critical content*. Your motivation to incorporate this strategy into your instructional toolbox may have come from a personal desire to improve your instructional practice through the implementation of a research-based set of strategies (such as those found in the Marzano teacher evaluation framework) or a desire to increase the rigor of the instructional strategies you implement in your class so that students meet the expectations of demanding standards such as the Common Core State Standards, Next Generation Science Standards, C3 Framework for Social Studies State Standards, or state standards based on or influenced by College and Career Readiness Anchor Standards.

This guide will help teachers of all grade levels and subjects improve their performance of a specific instructional strategy: *identifying critical content*. Narrowing your focus on a specific skill, such as *identifying critical content*, allows you to concentrate on the nuances of this instructional strategy in order to deliberately improve it. This allows you to intentionally plan, implement, monitor, adapt, and reflect on this single element of your instructional practice. A person seeking to become an expert displays distinctive behaviors, as explained by Marzano and Toth (2013):

- breaks down the specific skills required to be an expert

- focuses on improving those particular critical skill chunks (as opposed to easy tasks) during practice or day-to-day activities

- receives immediate, specific, and actionable feedback, particularly from a more experienced coach

- continually practices each critical skill at more challenging levels with the intention of mastering it, giving far less time to skills already mastered

This series of guides will support each of the above-listed behaviors, with a focus on breaking down the specific skills required to be an expert and giving day-to-day practical suggestions to enhance these skills.

## Building on the Marzano Instructional Framework

This series is based on the Marzano instructional framework, which is grounded in research and provides educators with the tools they need to connect instructional practice to student achievement. The series uses key terms that are specific to the Marzano model of instruction. Table 1 provides a glossary of these key terms.

**Table 1. Glossary of Key Terms**

| Term | Definition |
| --- | --- |
| CCSS | Common Core State Standards is the official name of the standards documents developed by the Common Core State Standards Initiative (CCSSI), the goal of which is to prepare America's students for college and career. |
| CCR | College and Career Readiness Anchor Standards are broad statements that incorporate individual standards for various grade levels and specific content areas. |
| Desired result | The intended result for the student(s) due to the implementation of a specific strategy. |
| Monitoring | The act of checking for evidence of the desired result of a specific strategy while the strategy is being implemented. |
| Instructional strategy | A category of techniques used for classroom instruction that has been proven to have a high probability of enhancing student achievement. |
| Instructional technique | The method used to teach and deepen understanding of knowledge and skills. |
| Content | The knowledge and skills necessary for students to demonstrate standards. |
| Scaffolding | A purposeful progression of support that targets cognitive complexity and student autonomy to reach rigor. |
| Extending | Activities that move students who have already demonstrated the desired result to a higher level of understanding. |

The educational pendulum swings widely from decade to decade. Educators move back and forth between prescriptive checklists and step-by-step lesson plans to approaches that encourage instructional autonomy with minimal regard for the science of teaching and need for accountability. Two practices are often missing in both of these approaches to defining effective instruction: 1) specific statements of desired results, and 2) solid research-based connections. The Marzano instructional framework provides a comprehensive system that details what is required from teachers to develop their craft using research-based instructional strategies. Launching from this solid instructional foundation, teachers will then be prepared to merge that science with their own unique, yet effective, instructional style, which is the art of teaching.

*Identifying Critical Content: Classroom Techniques to Help Students Know What Is Important* will help you grow into an innovative and highly skilled teacher who is able to implement, scaffold, and extend instruction to meet a range of student needs.

## Essentials for Achieving Rigor

This series of guides details essential classroom strategies to support the complex shifts in teaching that are necessary for an environment where academic rigor is a requirement for all students. The instructional strategies presented in this series are essential to effectively teach the CCSS, the Next Generation Science Standards, or standards designated by your school district or state. They require a deeper understanding, more effective use of strategies, and greater frequency of implementation for your students to demonstrate the knowledge and skills required by rigorous standards. This series includes instructional techniques appropriate for all grade levels and content areas. The examples contained within are grade-level specific and should serve as models and launching points for application in your own class.

Your skillful implementation of these strategies is essential to your students' mastery of the CCSS or other rigorous standards, no matter the grade level or subject matter you are teaching. Instructional strategies such as *Examining Reasoning* and *Engaging Students in Cognitively Complex Tasks* exemplify the cognitive complexity needed to meet rigorous standards. Taken as a package, these strategies may at first glance seem quite daunting. That is why this series focuses on just one strategy in each guide.

# Identifying Critical Content

In the context of teaching students brand new information, *identifying critical content* is one strategy you can't live without. As you become more skilled in this strategy, you will see remarkable changes in your students' abilities to process and understand new content because they are able to identify which content is critical and understand how learned content scaffolds in complexity. A classroom of scholars identifies critical content within standards, but also studies, recognizes, and celebrates as knowledge grows increasingly more sophisticated. Whether that standard is part of the CCSS or your district or state standards, your students will benefit from your expertise at identifying and conveying critical content to them. Take a moment to picture what you are preparing your students for: success in their future careers. In the workplace, information in constant competition for mental real estate will bombard your students. The skill of distinguishing critical information from that which is not critical is essential to a successful career. This instructional strategy reaches beyond helping students know what is critical in your classroom; it prepares them for a lifetime of being able to identify critical information.

The first step to helping your students know what is important is *identify a lesson, or part of a lesson, as involving important content to which students should pay particular attention.* This strategy is integral to helping your students understand new knowledge, make connections to prior learning, and ultimately retain new content. When implementing instructional strategies, teachers should identify and plan for the interdependence and cumulative effect among them. For example, once a teacher has *identified* the critical content, the next step is to *preview* the content with students, *chunk* that critical content, and ask students to *process* that content. After students have processed the content, teachers will ask questions that require students to make inferences, or *elaborate*, about content to further extend understanding. A teacher wanting to monitor whether students have internalized the critical content may ask them to record, represent, and reflect on this knowledge. The instructional strategies don't work in isolation, but a teacher with a broad instructional repertoire will skillfully blend the strategies in order to get overarching desired results. Although this guide will focus on *Identifying Critical Content*, it will also highlight the natural connections between this and other strategies, such as previewing and recording and representing.

There are many strategies that you can employ to intentionally teach content to students. The important attribute of *identifying critical content* is the role it plays when teaching something for the first time. Whenever you prepare to teach brand new knowledge, concepts, or skills that are likely to be unfamiliar to all or almost all of your students, communicate to them *why* the new learning is important; *how* it connects to their prior learning or experiences; and *when* the new knowledge will be necessary or beneficial.

## The Effective Implementation of Identifying Critical Content

Not all students are as savvy as teachers about what to do with important information. You must directly inform and specifically teach them. What are the ways you expect students to react to their awareness that critical information is forthcoming? What actions should they immediately take, such as writing new vocabulary in a journal or dictionary? Are there specific note-taking routines that were taught at the beginning of the school year and have been practiced to accuracy and automaticity? Do you expect students to give hand signals or write answers on small whiteboards to indicate their understanding of critical content? You cannot expect students to take action on important information unless you have stated and modeled your expectations and then followed up with consistent monitoring of their understanding of that information.

Effective communication of critical content requires adjustments in the way you present information to students. To make these adjustments, assemble a toolbox of ways to cue or prompt your students that you are about to introduce skills or knowledge of critical value and importance. Later in this guide you will find many ways to communicate the importance of critical content. As you read about the techniques, think about how to further develop those that are already your favorites, as well as how to become more skilled in employing different techniques to target subgroups of students that you may not currently be reaching.

The following behaviors are associated with identifying critical content:

- highlighting critical information that portrays a clear progression of information related to standards or goals

- identifying differences between critical and noncritical content

- continuously calling students' attention to critical content

- integrating cross curricular connections to critical content

As you learn to implement this strategy, think about how to avoid some common mistakes. These roadblocks can take your teaching and students' learning off course:

- You can fail to identify the critical content from a chapter, unit, or set of materials to read *before* you begin teaching.

- You can identify the critical content but then fail to communicate its importance to your students in effective and memorable ways that work best for the content or students.

- You can fail to communicate to students the kind of action or response their attention requires for certain types of important content.

### Failing to Correctly Identify Critical Content

Whether you are an elementary or secondary teacher, you can easily become more focused on subject matter you have taught for decades and overlook the teaching of a critically important skill that gives purpose to the knowledge. Your failure to identify the specific learning target or national standard for students may signal that you need a more comprehensive understanding of the standards and how they relate to your curriculum. Consider your purpose. Are you primarily using your class time to teach a skill or important information? Before the bell rings and you stand before your students, you must determine the important knowledge and skills you want to teach based on standards.

### Failing to Communicate the Importance of Critical Content in Effective Ways

Have you ever taken a class or listened to a lecture and at the end thought, "I'm not sure what I was supposed to learn or get out of this." If so, that may have been because the teacher or lecturer did not communicate the importance of critical content such that you were able to determine the key points. Not everything in a lesson is of equal importance. Some of our students inherently understand that, and some don't. Some of our students get bogged down in the minutiae of our lessons. Signaling to students what is critical in the content is key to implementing an effective lesson.

### Failing to Communicate the Type of Action Needed

After you have identified critical content and communicated its importance, do not neglect to give students opportunities to do something with this information. For example, if someone were to convince you of a certain key bit of information that is critical to your health, you are more inclined to figure out a way to remember that information. You might make a note of it or ask for additional information to clarify what is the most critical content. It is necessary to teach this skill to your students. Help them realize that hearing the critical content is only the first step; they need to do something with it for it to be effective.

## Monitoring for the Desired Result

Effective implementation means more than just applying the strategy—it also includes checking for evidence of the desired result of the specific strategy during implementation. In other words, effective implementation of a strategy includes monitoring for the desired result of that strategy in real time. Presenting a lively lesson that engages students is not enough. The questions that need to be answered are: Did your students know what content was important, and did they learn or master the information taught? The most elaborately planned lessons have no meaning unless they focus on the critical content outlined in standards and are monitored by the teacher for the desired results of the implemented strategies.

There are multiple ways teachers can monitor whether students know the content that is important and can distinguish between important and less significant information. Below are some examples that can help you tell if your students are able to identify critical content from a specific lesson:

1. Students can identify the critical information addressed in class.

2. Students can explain the difference between critical and noncritical content.

3.  Students can describe the level of importance of the critical information addressed in class.

4.  Formative data from the lesson show that students attend to the critical content (e.g., questioning, artifacts).

5.  Students can explain the progression of critical content in the lesson.

Each technique discussed in this guide also has examples of monitoring specific to that technique.

## Scaffolding and Extending Instruction to Meet Students' Needs

As you monitor for the desired result of each technique, you will probably realize that some students are not able to identify the critical content and others are easily able to demonstrate the desired result of the strategy. With this knowledge, it becomes necessary to adapt for the needs of your students. You must plan ahead of time for those students who may need you to scaffold or extend instruction to meet their needs.

There are four different categories of support you can provide for students who need scaffolding: 1) support that teachers (including instructional aides or other paraprofessionals) or peers provide; 2) support that teachers provide by manipulating the difficulty level of content that is being taught (for example, providing an easier reading level that contains the same content); 3) breaking down the content into smaller chunks to make it more manageable; and 4) giving students organizers or think sheets to clarify and guide their thinking through a task one step at a time (Dickson, Collins, Simmons, & Kame'enui, 1998).

Within each technique that is described in subsequent chapters, there are illustrative examples of ways to scaffold and extend instruction to meet the needs of your students. Scaffolding provides support that targets cognitive complexity and student autonomy to reach rigor. Extending moves students who have already demonstrated the desired result to a higher level of understanding. These examples are provided as suggestions and should be adapted to target the specific needs of your students. Use the scaffolding examples to spark ideas as you plan to meet the needs of your English language learners, students who receive special education or lack support, or simply the student who was absent the day before. The extension activities can help you plan for students in your gifted and talented program or those with a keen interest in the subject matter you are teaching who have already learned the fundamentals.

## Teacher Self-Reflection

As you work on your expertise in teaching students to identify critical content, reflecting on what works and doesn't work can help you become more successful in the implementation of this strategy. Use the following set of reflection questions to guide you. The questions begin with reflecting about how to begin the implementation process and move to progressively more complex ways of helping students identify critical content.

1. How can you begin to incorporate some aspect of this strategy in your instruction?

2. How can you signal to students which content is critical versus non-critical?

3. How could you monitor the extent to which students attend to critical content?

4. What are some ways you can adapt and create new techniques for identifying critical information that addresses unique student needs and situations?

5. What are you learning about your students as you adapt and create new techniques?

## Instructional Techniques to Help Students Identify Critical Content

There are many ways to help your students effectively interact with new knowledge and ultimately master the learning targets or standards of the grade level or content area. The ways you choose to put your students on high alert regarding critical content that is about to unfold during a specific lesson or unit will depend on your grade, content, and the makeup of your class. These various ways or options are called instructional techniques. In the following pages, you will find descriptions of how to implement the following techniques:

1. Verbally cue critical content.

2. Use explicit instruction to convey critical content.

3. Use dramatic instruction to convey critical content.

4. Provide advance organizers to cue critical content.

5. Visually cue critical content.

6. Use storytelling to cue critical content.

7. Use what students already know to cue critical content.

All of the techniques are similarly organized and include the following components:

- a brief introduction to the technique

- ways to effectively implement the technique

- common mistakes to avoid as you implement the technique

- examples and nonexamples from elementary and secondary classrooms using selected learning targets or standards from various documents

- ways to monitor for the desired result

- ways to scaffold and extend instruction to meet the needs of students

# Instructional Technique 1

# VERBALLY CUE CRITICAL CONTENT

The easiest, and often fastest, way to communicate to your students that certain information is important is to tell them. That is the essence of verbal cueing. This sounds simple enough until you realize, after teaching a concept or skill, that your students' questions indicate they do not understand what is important about the lesson even though you taught it. There is an effective way to convey critical information to students. This instructional technique, verbal cueing, will help you effectively implement the strategy of identifying critical content.

## How to Effectively Implement Verbal Cueing

The effective execution of verbal cueing depends largely on the accurate identification of the important information in the content you are teaching. Use prioritized standards and learning targets to identify the critical content in a unit, lesson, and digestible bite of information. Use resources to ensure accuracy of the critical content, and then plan for how you will cue its importance to your students. Here are three ways you can verbally cue critical content.

### Directly State the Important Information

Be direct, succinct, and assertive in stating the information that is important. If you feel overwhelmed by the amount of information you think should be included in your lesson, imagine how some of your students will feel. Take a moment to identify the central idea and a few supporting details, and work with that structure to determine how you will state which information is important.

### Raise or Lower Your Voice to Indicate Critical Content

Students take cues from your intonation. Leverage that to signal to students what is important about the information you are imparting. Raise or lower your voice for a few sentences to help students focus on critical content. This may take practice; don't hesitate to record yourself as part of learning to implement this technique.

### Pause at Key Points During the Presentation

The simple act of pausing at key points during a presentation of new content gives students time to think about information and signal what they find to be important. This enhances their ability to identify the critical content in a lesson.

## Common Mistakes

Learning from mistakes while trying to teach is often painful. Knowing ahead of time where problems might arise will increase your likelihood of success in implementing this technique. Watch out for these common mistakes when you use verbal cueing:

- The teacher has a difficult time isolating the critical content, which results in making general statements instead of cueing critical content.

- The teacher uses a verbal cue too frequently, causing students to feel confused and overwhelmed by the sheer volume of important information.

- The teacher might pause for emphasis too frequently or sustain the pauses for too long a time, leaving students unable to determine the critical content.

- The teacher inconsistently changes intonation and seems to signal that information is important when it isn't.

### Examples of Verbal Cueing in the Classroom

Following are two examples (one elementary and one secondary) and their corresponding nonexamples of verbal cueing. As you read, think about experiences you have had in your classroom. Consider the common mistakes and note how the example teachers cleverly avoid them and the nonexample teachers miss the mark by making one of these common mistakes.

*Elementary Example of Verbal Cueing*

The first example/nonexample illustrates verbal cueing when introducing critical information about the skill of listening at the elementary level. The standard is taken from the CCSS Speaking and Listening Standards for Grades K–5: *follow agreed-upon rules for discussions (for example, listening to others and taking turns speaking about the topics and texts under discussion)* (CCSS, Speaking and Listening Standards K–5, p. 23). In the example, the teacher begins with "listening to others" and identifies two pieces of critical information about the listening skill. The bold text indicates where the teacher changes the pitch of his voice to indicate that critical content follows.

> Good morning, class. Today we are going to learn how to listen. One important thing about listening is that **you do not talk when you are listening.** The second important thing about listening is that **you should look at the person who is talking to you.** You are listening to me right now. I can tell because **you are not talking** and **you are looking at me.**

After this brief introduction, the teacher goes on to teach the rest of the lesson. He first solicits some student volunteers to demonstrate the two important things about listening: not talking, and looking at the person who is talking to you. In this example, listening is a new skill the teacher wants his students to learn. He will use the verbal cueing he used for the introductory lesson as a reminder whenever he asks students to talk to a partner.

*Elementary Nonexample of Verbal Cueing*

The following elementary nonexample is based on the same grade level and CCSS listening standard as the previous example.

> Good morning, class. I thought we'd talk about **listening** today. I hope when we get done with our lesson you'll know how to be a good listener. Listening is really an important thing to do in school. I know you all know that because you're sitting so quietly and being such good listeners now. I want you to practice listening today. I have some stickers here, and whenever I see a good listener during the day, I'm going to silently give that person a sticker.

The nonexample teacher doesn't actually identify the critical content for the skill of listening. The teacher fails to focus on what is important and makes general statements instead. In this scenario, there is no indication of what is critical about listening. Before you teach a lesson, summarize the content in a sentence or two. This is the critical content you need to cue to students.

### Verbal Cueing in the Secondary Classroom

The secondary example/nonexample is also based on a speaking and listening standard. It is the CCR Anchor Standard 1 for Speaking and Listening that expects students to *prepare for and participate effectively in a range of conversations and collaborations with diverse partners, building on others' ideas and expressing their own clearly and persuasively.*

### Secondary Example of Verbal Cueing

This example features a high school social studies teacher who is trying to teach his students a specific aspect of Standard 1: *come to discussions prepared, having read and researched material under study.* He wants to convey the important information about the task in a brief lesson using verbal cueing. The bold text indicates that the teacher is raising or lowering his voice to emphasize two items of critical importance that he wants his students to take away from the lesson.

> Greetings, class. Today we are going to think and talk about what it means to **prepare for** and **participate in** a discussion. There are two important things to remember from this lesson today. Write them in your academic notebook. The first important thing is that **preparing means doing something positive ahead of time to get ready for the discussion.** The second important thing is that **participation means actively doing something positive during the class discussion.**

After this verbal cue, the teacher divides the class into small groups. Half of the groups list as many answers as they can to this question: What are some positive things you could do to prepare for class? The other set of groups lists answers to this question: What are some positive things you should do during the class discussion to show that you are participating? The teacher walks around looking at the list of activities that each small group has generated and concludes that students can identify the importance of preparing and participating.

### Secondary Nonexample of Verbal Cueing

The nonexample secondary teacher begins his lesson the same way as the example teacher. Take careful note of where this teacher makes two common mistakes, thereby missing the opportunity to check that the desired result of this instructional technique was achieved.

> Greetings, class. Today we are going to think and talk about what it means to prepare for and participate in a discussion. There are two things to remember from this lesson today. Write them in your academic notebook right now. The first important thing is that **preparing means doing something ahead of time to get ready for the discussion.** The second important thing is that **participation means actively doing something during the class discussion.**

Tomorrow, I want everyone to come prepared to partici-pate in the class discussion about chapter two. Remember, part of your grade in this class depends on preparing and participating.

The nonexample teacher left out two important pieces of his lesson: 1) giving students opportunities to do something with the important infor-mation, and 2) monitoring whether students understood the two pieces of critical content.

## Determining If Students Can Identify Critical Content from Verbal Cueing

Always take time to monitor whether students know the difference between important and unimportant content. To find out who knows and how well they know it, assemble a toolkit of tasks designed to fit your grade or content area. Here is a collection of ways that you can monitor your students' under-standing of critical content as a result of verbal cueing:

- Students indicate their answer to a question from one of two or more possible answers by holding up color-coded cards. For example, stu-dents may display one of two response cards: Yes or No. The teacher notes students who have made incorrect choices, and plans to follow up with them.

- Students keep journals or learning logs in which they write entries on the critical information from each lesson in a particular unit. They leave them open on top of their desks so the teacher can scan them for the critical content.

- Students write their answers to questions or problems on small white-boards and hold them up for the teacher to read.

- Students respond chorally. The teacher notes the students who respond incorrectly and makes a mental note that these students will need more opportunities to respond. The teacher takes care to ensure that all students respond and can be heard.

Use the student proficiency scale for verbal cueing to determine the progression of your students' ability to identify critical content. Explain to them why some information is important and why other information is irrelevant or trivial.

**Student Proficiency Scale for Verbally Cueing Critical Content**

| Emerging | Fundamental | Desired Result |
|---|---|---|
| Students can state what the lesson is about. | Students can state some, but not all, of the important information in the lesson. | Students successfully state the important information in the lesson. |
| Students can list some information in the lesson that is important. | Students can explain which information in the lesson is important versus unimportant. | Students accurately explain why some information in the lesson is important versus unimportant. |

## Scaffold and Extend Instruction to Meet Students' Needs

As you become more skilled at identifying critical content and using verbal cues to convey information, you will find that you can more readily identify various individuals or small groups of students who need something more or different from your original instruction. Some students need support, or scaffolding, that takes them from where they are to where they need to be. Other students need to be challenged further, so you must extend the ways in which you expect them to interact with critical content. The following suggestions are meant to be illustrative. Use them as springboards for zeroing in on the precise needs of your students.

### Scaffolding

Instructional support for verbal cueing may take the form of further explanations, more vocabulary instruction and guided practice, or teacher modeling. Use your classroom walls to provide scaffolding for students. Post resources that students can consult—such as a word wall, picture keys, or important steps in a process—to identify critical content.

## Extending

Think about extension activities for your students who have readily mastered identifying important and unimportant information and can manipulate the critical content at higher levels. This will enlarge and deepen their knowledge. Two ways to extend students' interaction with critical content is to ask them to either prioritize or categorize the critical information of the lesson.

# USE EXPLICIT INSTRUCTION TO CONVEY CRITICAL CONTENT

If you are unaware of the power of explicit instruction to convey complex concepts and information to students, *or* if you have made a conscious decision to avoid any instructional approach that might be perceived as too direct, you owe it to your students to be more explicit. When the information or skill is foundational and there is no room for failure, consider using explicit instruction. If students are struggling, lack background knowledge or vocabulary, or have special needs, explicit instruction is essential. The more explicitly you teach critical content, the more readily all of your students can apply what they have learned. Lay out important information and skills in plain language that leaves no confusion in your students' minds.

## How to Effectively Implement Explicit Instruction

### Explicitly Identify the Critical Content

Point out to students what's important in the content. Even if you're pressed for time or think students should know what's important in the lesson based on previous lessons, you must explicitly identify the critical content of each chunk of information and for each lesson. If your notes are in slide form, consider preparing at least one slide in which you state the critical content for every lesson. Explicit instruction should be simple, plain, clear, and systematic. It should focus on the critical content and be free of irrelevant bells and whistles that may distract students.

### Model Critical Skills, Strategies, and Processes

Modeling is one of the most effective ways to communicate critical content. It can take several forms in your classroom:

- Demonstrate or show your students explicitly how to perform a skill, strategy, or process.

- Think aloud as you perform the skill, strategy, or process.

- Show exemplars of completed student work, as well as nonexamples, that help your students differentiate between good and unacceptable work.

## Chunk Critical Content into Digestible Bites

Students need time to think as they are learning. If you race through material, students don't have opportunities to process and take ownership of the content. Learning proceeds more efficiently when students receive information in small chunks that they can process immediately. There is no set rule for how large or small a chunk should be, but usually the more students know about the content, the larger the chunk can be. Use the following suggestions to present digestible bites of information:

- Present only one important concept or idea at a time.

- After presenting new information, give students thinking time in which they may talk with a partner, write out a question, or write an answer on a small whiteboard.

- Design handouts so that all of the information students need is on one page.

- Pass out only one handout at a time.

- Give only one direction at a time.

## Develop Student-Friendly Definitions for Important Concepts

Student-friendly definitions distill a concept to its essence using simple words that students are more likely to understand and remember. Explicit instruction requires consistent and easy-to-understand definitions. Extend the consistency to all classes within a grade level or all content courses in a department to give students increased opportunities to practice and master these definitions.

# Common Mistakes

Teachers want *all* students to master the required content and skills. Explicit instruction is one way to ensure that students who may be struggling with the basics have an opportunity to acquire them to the same extent as those students who catch on quickly. The latter group of students may readily compensate even if a teacher stumbles during instruction; however, struggling students need every teacher's A-game in order to achieve mastery. Watch out for these common mistakes when you use explicit instruction:

- The teacher provides vague or general information.

- The teacher moves too quickly or laboriously long through the introduction of critical information, minimizing the amount of explicit instruction.

- The teacher assumes that students have prior knowledge they do not have.

- The teacher doesn't give students opportunities to write down, talk with a partner, or ask questions about digestible bites of important information.

- The teacher's presentation style distracts students from the critical content.

## Examples and Nonexamples of Explicit Instruction

As you consider these examples and nonexamples, read carefully to recognize the common mistakes and make connections to the suggestions for how to effectively implement explicit instruction.

### Elementary Example of Explicit Instruction

The first example focuses on the standard: *demonstrate basic knowledge of one-to-one letter-sound correspondences by producing the primary or many of the most frequent sounds for each consonant* (CCSS Reading Standards: Foundational Skills K–5, p. 16). The example teacher is teaching one consonant at a time. A formative assessment showed that most students in the class do not associate the /s/ sound with the letter *s*. So the teacher has chosen to provide explicit instruction on the /s/ sound.

> Today we're going to learn a new sound. Our new sound goes with the letter **s.** I'm going to make the sound for you, and then you will have many turns to practice the sound. When you know the sounds that go with the letters, you will be able to read words and books. Listen to what I say and watch my lips.
>
> Here's our new sound for today. *Teacher points to the **s** on the board.* The letter says /s/.
>
> *The teacher points to the letter and says:* Together. What sound? /s/ Yes.

The teacher and students repeat this segment several times while the teacher watches students' eyes and mouths to see if any of them are having difficulty. In the next phase of the lesson, the students respond in unison without the teacher's support. In this type of explicit instruction, only one sound at a time is introduced and then practiced to mastery.

### Elementary Nonexample of Explicit Instruction

Our nonexample of explicit instruction is also focused on learning letter-sound correspondence for the letter *s*.

> I have a wonderful new story to read aloud to you. *Teacher holds up book titled **Sam's Silly Sister Sue**. Can someone tell me what they see on the front cover? Students point out that there is a girl roller-skating. A fluffy dog and little boy are laughing at her. Students agree that Sam is the boy, the girl is sister Sue, and the dog is probably named Spot.*

The teacher is excited about all of the information the children have inferred from the picture. At this point, she has yet to introduce the most important information of this lesson: the connection between the printed letter and sound it makes. She goes on to ask students to signal a thumbs-up whenever they hear the sound that the letter *s* makes while she is reading the story aloud to them.

This teacher has made a couple common mistakes. First, she provides vague information. She also assumes that the students have the prior knowledge to determine the relationship between the letter *s* and its sound from her read-aloud.

### Secondary Example of Explicit Instruction

The secondary example is from a high school geology class. The learning target for students comes from the first section of Standard 1 of the College and Career Readiness Anchor Standards for Reading. It states that students are expected to *read closely to determine what the text says explicitly.* Explicit instruction in the context of this standard calls for explicit modeling and thinking aloud by the teacher. The teacher's modeling will give students an accessible way to understand how skilled readers extract meaning.

Today we're going to learn what it means to read closely to determine what a text says explicitly. I'm going to show you a three-step way to do that. *The teacher puts a paragraph relating to geology on the screen. The teacher has already determined that many of his students have great difficulty figuring out what a text is explicitly about, so he decided to provide the students with a question to guide their reading and thinking.*

I often find it hard to read something long and complicated while at the same time trying to remember what I've read. Today I am going to show you how to read one sentence at a time to see if it answers a question. The question is, What does the text explicitly say caused the land surface of the earth to change? **The first step is reading one sentence. The second step is deciding if the sentence answers the question.** Let me show you how it works. *Teacher reads aloud the first sentence of the text and rereads the question.* As I read this sentence, I don't find anything that tells me a reason or a cause for the earth to change. So, I would answer no. This sentence does not answer the question. **The third step is explaining why the sentence doesn't answer the question.** I say that the first sentence told us what the paragraph would be about, but it didn't give any reasons for why the earth changed.

The teacher continues to model this process for students with the next sentence before asking students to try one by themselves.

*Secondary Nonexample of Explicit Instruction*

Today we're going to cover the first chapter in our new unit about how the earth's surface has changed over time. I want you to really concentrate when you read this first section. You need to get every bit of meaning out of it that's there so you will be able to write a one-sentence summary that answers this question: What does the text explicitly say caused the land surface of the earth to change?

The teacher provides no modeling. He expects students to read the whole text and write a summary rather than chunking the reading into digestible bites. Many students may be unable to accomplish this.

## Determining If Students Can Identify Critical Content from Explicit Instruction

Monitoring students' abilities to identify the critical content from the scripted type of explicit instruction found in the elementary example is quite simple. The constant back and forth between the teacher and class during periods of unison response offers constant opportunities to monitor students. As you become more adept at eliciting whole-group responses, you can begin to call randomly on individual students. This kind of random questioning serves two purposes: 1) it keeps all students engaged and anticipating the next question, and 2) it gives students who are still uncertain about the critical content an opportunity to hear the correct response.

When a student gives an incorrect response, don't be reluctant to correct him or her by quickly modeling the correct answer and moving on. Come back to that student again to give him or her an opportunity to answer correctly. You can implement this kind of monitoring in just a few seconds and use it to check recall of critical information from prior lessons. The call and response between you and your students can help create a classroom climate where errors are merely momentary setbacks.

Monitoring students' abilities to identify critical content from the explicit instruction of comprehension skills, such as in the secondary example, depends on the quality and frequency of thinking aloud and modeling you provide for them. When you make your thinking transparent, students will follow your lead and soon be comfortable with sharing their thoughts about what they have read. This is the most effective kind of monitoring to determine if students have isolated the critical content. Plan how and when you will provide opportunities for students to share their thoughts with a partner or the whole class, so that you can listen in and check that they know what content is critical.

Use the student proficiency scale for explicit instruction to determine whether your students are demonstrating the desired results as you implement this technique. Make a copy for reference as you plan and implement explicit instruction in your class.

**Student Proficiency Scale for Explicit Instruction**

| Emerging | Fundamental | Desired Result |
|---|---|---|
| Students provide responses related to the important information in the lesson. | Students provide accurate responses regarding the important information in the lesson. | Students provide comprehensive, accurate responses regarding the important information in the lesson. |
| Students can state some critical content. | Students are able to discuss the critical content. | Students are able to successfully process the critical content. |

# Scaffold and Extend Instruction to Meet Students' Needs

Meeting the needs of your students may require designing lessons for both your struggling and your higher achieving students to become more self-managed in your classroom. Below are some examples of each.

## Scaffolding

When you are having difficulty with individuals or a small group of students who do not seem to grasp or remember the critical information from day to day, or even in the same day, try one of the following ways to adjust your instruction:

- Remind, review, and reteach critical content that students need more frequently (for example, important academic vocabulary).

- Provide a classroom or subject matter reference book that contains frequently used vocabulary or spelling words, rules, procedures, and checklists for students to consult if they are confused.

- Develop specific and consistent classroom routines to identify critical content so that students recognize the cues.

## Extending

Some of your students may need an extra challenge to make identifying critical content enhance their learning for that lesson. Try these ideas for extending explicit instruction:

- Encourage students who are able to quickly parse important information to rank it in order of significance.

- Ask students who are proficient in identifying critical content to create a cheat sheet that includes the critical content and what led them to know it was critical. This can then be used to help students who are not as proficient with this process.

# Instructional Technique 3

# USE DRAMATIC INSTRUCTION TO CONVEY CRITICAL CONTENT

Students who have a difficult time acquiring new knowledge from other ways of identifying critical content may benefit from acting out the critical content. This does not need to entail formal scripts and long-winded speeches. Students acting out math facts or linking hand signals to key vocabulary are types of dramatic instruction.

## How to Effectively Implement Dramatic Instruction

There are several types of dramatic instruction from which to choose. They include role plays, skits, dramatic readings, hand gestures, and coordinated movements such as dance. Here are the key aspects to remember as you plan your lesson.

### Choose Just One Type of Dramatic Instruction

If you have a flair for the dramatic and coach the after-school drama club, you may be tempted to combine several types of dramatic instruction mentioned earlier. Remember that your goal is to signal to students the importance of the material being presented—not to mount a full-scale production.

### Check Alignment to the Learning Target

Class time is too precious to spend time on dramatic instruction that doesn't tie to the critical content, no matter how fun it is. If you are unsure about the overt linkage between the dramatic instruction and critical content, run your idea past a colleague. Explain exactly what you propose to do and how it connects to the content. If you aren't able to make a case, it is best to abandon the idea and find another.

### Rehearse, Rehearse, Rehearse

Walk through how your lesson will work in the real world of your classroom. If your students have never used physical movement to illustrate word meanings, you will need to model an example or two for them. Establish some routines for dramatic instruction such as personal space and movement around the classroom. Take care to rehearse several times to decide where and when you will use your voice and body and how long the dramatization will be.

### Students Need to Summarize

Be sure to include an opportunity for your student to explain how the enactment represents the critical content. Otherwise you might find that some students were successful in the enactment but do not understand how the enactment ties to the lesson.

### The More Students Involved, the Better

There is sometimes the temptation to call on the exceptionally talented students to participate in a skit. This may cause most students to love the performance, but fail to interact with the new knowledge you want them to master. Whenever possible, instead of only modeling the dramatic instruction, have all students participate.

## Common Mistakes

There are a few common mistakes teachers make as they use dramatic instruction to convey critical information:

- The teacher does not make overt linkages between the performance or dramatization and critical content.

- The teacher involves only a few students in the dramatization. Students who are watching are not likely to acquire the critical content to the same extent as those who are acting, moving, or demonstrating with face, hands, or body.

- The teacher demonstrates everything and does not ask students to participate at all. This does not give all students the benefits of dramatic instruction.

- The teacher does not ask students to summarize the performance. This mistake means that some students may not make the linkage between the dramatization and the critical content.

## Examples and Nonexamples of Dramatic Instruction

Some of these examples may be from a different grade level or subject than you teach. View them as you would a fresh perspective from a colleague, and use them to find a new approach or alternative way of thinking about instruction.

### Elementary Example of Dramatic Instruction

The first example and nonexample illustrate how and how not to use dramatic instruction to teach vocabulary in a classroom with students who need extra support in learning English language vocabulary.

The specific standard being addressed is *distinguishing shades of meaning among verbs differing in manner or intensity by defining or choosing them or by acting out the meanings* (CCSS, Language Standards K–5, p. 27). The teacher has chosen this set of words to use dramatic instruction for the first time with her students: *look, peek, glance, stare, glare,* and *scowl.* In this lesson, students will act out the meanings of the words. The teacher posted cues on a bulletin board for students to consult. The dramatic instruction has scaffolding and extending built in such that struggling students will have a third opportunity to master the word meanings by adding the right facial expressions or hand movements (if needed), while advanced students will be challenged to write a short play that incorporates both the words and facial expressions.

> *The students are sitting on a rug in front of an easel that contains a list of the words with their meanings, as well as their picture cues.*
>
> On Monday we began to learn some new words. The words, meanings, and picture cues to help you remember the meanings are here on the easel. Today we're going to add one more thing to each word to help us remember what it means. We're going to act out the words. Let me show you what I mean.

> *The teacher points to the word* peek, *pronounces it, points to the picture cue, and reads the meaning. Then she acts out the meaning of the word* peek *for her students.* Everybody show me what *peek* looks like. Terrific. I was peeking at my students. Who were you peeking at? *The students answer, "The teacher."*
>
> I'm going to act out another word. *The teacher acts out the word* scowl, *and then reads the word and its meaning.* I was scowling at you. But it was just a pretend scowl because I am not angry with you. Now, everybody show me what your *scowl* looks like. Excellent. Now show me what a *peek* looks like. I'm going to point at the word, and I want you to show me the face that goes with it.

All of the students in the group can produce dramatic facial expressions to match the words *peek* and *scowl*. The instruction gets more dramatic as the students begin to acquire the subtleties of this set of words and become more comfortable in pronouncing the words and producing the definitions in English. The teacher checks throughout the lesson that students can match facial expressions to their corresponding words, as well as read them on the chart and produce a spoken meaning for each word.

### Elementary Nonexample of Dramatic Instruction

The nonexample elementary teacher has the same general plan as the example teacher, but she misses the mark at a crucial point in the lesson. Her students never get to try out any of the faces, and she stops the lesson without monitoring the students' abilities to match the appropriate facial expressions with the words and meanings on the chart.

### Secondary Example of Dramatic Instruction

The secondary example and nonexample are from a high school biology class. It focuses on the Next Generation Science Standard HS-LS1-4: *use a model to illustrate the role of cellular division (mitosis) and differentiation in producing and maintaining complex organisms.* The high school biology teacher in this example will have her students develop a simulation of mitosis to help them understand the process of cell division.

The teacher begins by giving students time to review their notes and activities from previous lessons in which they learned about the purpose and process of mitosis. Rather than memorizing each step of the process, students in small groups brainstorm how they can act out the process of mitosis, focusing on the obstacles that cells overcome in order to reproduce. As students are creating their enactment, the teacher walks around listening and giving guidance when necessary. Instead of asking each group to demonstrate to the entire class, the teacher has them partner with one other group. In addition to enacting mitosis, the groups summarize how the model illustrates the role of mitosis in producing and maintaining complex organisms.

### Secondary Nonexample of Dramatic Instruction

The nonexample teacher plans a similar lesson, but instead of asking students to brainstorm their own enactment, she guides a small group of students through the enactment while the rest of the class watches. This is an equally effective simulation but fails to follow through with the most important phase of instruction—involving the students and monitoring that they understand the process of mitosis and are able to summarize how the model illustrates the role of mitosis in producing and maintaining complex organisms.

## Determining If Students Can Identify Critical Content from Dramatic Instruction

Monitoring should always have two components: 1) something that students do to demonstrate the desired result of the technique (in this instance, state the critical content depicted in the dramatic instruction); and 2) something that the teacher does to check for the desired result and respond to students' progress. Here are some specific examples of monitoring that flow from the use of dramatic instruction:

- Students summarize the dramatic reading or skit to a partner. Meanwhile, the teacher quickly moves about the room and listens to the spoken summaries to ensure that students have identified the critical content.

- Students add a quick sketch of the hand gestures to their notes to match the corresponding critical content; the teacher checks that they are able to match the gestures to the content.

- Students narrate the coordinated body movements using critical content from the lesson, and the teacher confirms that the students' narrations link the body movements and critical content.

The student proficiency scale for dramatic instruction shows the range of student proficiencies for how successfully they can use dramatic instruction cues to master the critical content of a specific lesson. Use the scale to reflect the precise ways you plan to identify the desired result of dramatic instruction.

**Student Proficiency Scale for Dramatic Instruction of Critical Content**

| Emerging | Fundamental | Desired Result |
|---|---|---|
| Students participate in the dramatization. | Students can explain how the dramatization relates to the lesson. | Students are able to relate the dramatization to the critical content of the lesson. |
| Students can identify some critical content in the dramatization. | Students can discuss the dramatization using some of the critical content. | Students can correctly narrate the dramatization using critical content. |
| Students can discuss parts of the dramatization. | Students can make statements about the critical content in the dramatization. | Students can accurately summarize the critical content in the dramatization. |
| Students can state some critical content. | | |

# Scaffold and Extend Instruction to Meet Students' Needs

There will be students who do not grasp critical information the first time they hear it. Similarly, there are students who "get it" and "had it" before you "taught" it. Meeting the needs of these two diverse groups of students requires that you adapt your instruction. The more focused a teacher is on designing instruction for all students, the more ground he or she will gain with students on either end of the achievement continuum. Here are some ideas for developing scaffolding and extending to meet students' needs.

## Scaffolding

- If students struggle with extracting the critical content from dramatic instruction, create sentences that relate to the dramatic instruction. Write some that contain critical content and some that do not. Ask students to sort the statements into two groups: important and not important.

- Some students may struggle with drawing pictures of the hand gestures you introduced as part of the lesson. Provide these students with small pictures of these hand gestures that they may tape into their notes or use as a model to copy.

- If students did not make the linkage between your dramatic instruction and the critical content, ask some questions to help them understand the connection.

## Extending

- Have students create an original skit, dramatic reading, set of hand gestures, or a set of dance moves to convey the critical content.

- Ask students to evaluate the work of classmates to select the best example that illustrates the critical content and justify that decision.

## Instructional Technique 4

# PROVIDE ADVANCE ORGANIZERS TO CUE CRITICAL CONTENT

An advance man (or woman) is someone who travels ahead of a main attraction, stirring up interest and promoting attendance. In the olden days, an advance man arrived before the circus to put up posters all over town and create a sense of anticipation and desire among the younger set. Today, advance men and women arrive before politicians to ensure enthusiastic crowds of supporters.

Psychologist David Ausubel (1960) coined the phrase *advance organizer* to describe the ways teachers can help students activate prior knowledge and experience, connect it to new learning, and then retain concepts and information from classroom presentations. The term *advance organizer* has acquired multiple meanings, as it has been interpreted since Ausubel first introduced the phrase. It can be used to describe a nonlinguistic representation of a concept, or it can consist solely of spoken words.

A teacher may use either a nonlinguistic or linguistically focused organizer to assist students in identifying and organizing their thoughts around what is critical and what is not. Using an advance organizer is a technique to cue the critical information in the upcoming lesson. An artful teacher may use techniques, such as advance organizers, prior to identifying critical content or after identifying critical content to make the previewing connections even stronger. For instance, a teacher may verbally identify three central targets of a lesson and then use an advance organizer to make explicit connections between prior knowledge and learning targets.

# How to Effectively Implement Advance Organizers

The following steps to effectively implement advance organizers are meant to be suggestive. Do not interpret them as a must-do checklist. Consider your strengths as a teacher, the needs of your students, and the specific nature of the lesson you are teaching to focus on the steps that work best for your context.

## Define the Scope of Your Organizer

Following are various approaches you might take in designing your advance organizer. Don't attempt to do more than one in case students lose sight of the critical content.

### Give Students the Big Picture

If you are beginning a new unit of instruction that has many components, design your organizer to give students an overview, or big picture, of that unit. For example, you might provide an organizer that contains frames on which students can write critical content day by day. Or, you might choose to develop a concept map on a large whiteboard on which students take turns filling in various pieces of critical content weekly. The big picture you provide in your initial advance organizer can serve as a reference throughout the duration of the unit.

### Build Connections to the Past and for the Future

One of the most powerful ways to use an advance organizer is to connect new learning to previous learning, and show students how the new knowledge and skills will serve them in the future. Effective teachers take every opportunity they can to help students fill in the big picture with the critical content they learn day by day.

### Choose a Metaphor to Organize Teaching and Learning

Well-chosen metaphors can help students hang on to critical content over the course of many weeks and months. Try using metaphors such as the hard drive of a computer for your students' retention of critical content; a toolkit for a set of strategies for problem solving; or a detective or investigative reporter for reading or writing.

### Keep Your Organizer Simple

The overriding purpose of an advance organizer is to convey critical content about a lesson. An advance organizer can serve other purposes nicely, but resist the temptation to overload your organizer with too much information, or students will not know which information is critical.

### Present the Material

There are many ways to present critical content in an advance organizer. The simplest is to state the critical content and explain to students why they need to know it. Also, consider asking students how critical content connects to their lives.

### Adapt the Organizer for Your Context

Some of your students may know a great deal about the content and organizer, but some may not. Explain why you chose a certain organizer and how to use it. Use your knowledge of your students and subject matter to design the advance organizer that works best for your context.

### Be Disciplined in Your Delivery

Remind students of the big picture. Link the critical content of the lesson to what they already know. Reiterate key vocabulary. But during all this, remember that the purpose of an advance organizer is to help students focus on critical content. If you try to do too much with it, you may make it hard for students to distinguish what is important from what isn't.

## Common Mistakes

Most teachers have experienced the sinking feeling that comes from getting off on the wrong foot during a lesson. It's always better if we can learn from others' mistakes and avoid that feeling as often as possible. The most common mistakes to avoid when using advance organizers include the following:

- The teacher overwhelms students with information such that they are unable to determine the critical content.

- The teacher assumes that students have prior knowledge they do not have.

- The teacher develops an advance organizer that is too broad and does not focus on the critical content of the lesson.

- The teacher creates an advance organizer that does not address the critical content.

- The teacher develops an advance organizer that lacks structure or is structured incoherently.

- The teacher designs an advance organizer that is not applicable to students' developmental levels.

## Examples and Nonexamples of Advance Organizers

The following examples and nonexamples demonstrate the introduction of advance organizers.

### Elementary Example of Using an Advance Organizer

The learning target being addressed is taken from the CCSS Writing Standards for Grades K–5: *students write opinion pieces in which they introduce the topic or name the book they are writing about, state an opinion, supply the reason for the opinion, and provide some sense of closure.* In the example, the teacher begins with the phrase *state an opinion* and identifies two critical pieces of information related to that task. The teacher has developed the organizer as a way to present an academic challenge to her students while at the same time conveying the critical content.

> Today we are going to learn how to give an opinion. Here is what's important for you to know about giving an opinion: **An opinion is what you think of something. Giving your opinion is telling someone what you think of something.** For example, I have an opinion about a movie I saw this weekend. Remember that my opinion is what I think of the movie, not what the movie is about. I would be giving my opinion, or what I thought of the movie, such as it was really funny!

*Elementary Nonexample of Using an Advance Organizer*

The nonexample is based on the same grade level and learning target: stating an opinion.

> I saw the movie *Frozen* this weekend and it was terrible. *Many children quickly shout out their disagreement with the teacher's opinion.* Now wait a minute, I was just stating my opinion. I can see that all of you have different opinions. And we all have a right to our opinions.

The nonexample teacher made the common mistake of overwhelming students with information. They are focused on their own opinions rather than learning about other opinions. Students are vocalizing their opinions of the movie before the teacher has even conveyed the critical information: *what an opinion is and how to give an opinion.* Some of the students may have prior knowledge about giving opinions, but those who don't could easily conclude that this was a new part of the morning routine—talking about the movies everyone saw over the weekend.

*Secondary Example of Using an Advance Organizer*

The secondary example and nonexample are based on the learning target *construct an explanation based on evidence for how the availability of natural resources has influenced human activity.* They feature a high school science teacher who is teaching how to write arguments on discipline-specific content. Students will work on how to *introduce precise claim(s), distinguish the claim(s) from alternate or opposing claims, and create an organization that establishes clear relationships among the claim(s), counterclaims, reasons, and evidence based on a corresponding CCSS Literacy Standard.* The teacher decides that the advance organizer will not only serve the primary purpose of conveying critical information related to the skill, but also show how this critical information will serve the students in the future.

Today we are going to take the first step in learning how to write arguments focused on how the availability of natural resources has influenced human activity. I am going to be modeling the various steps in the process for you. Your assignment today is to understand three important terms: claim, reason, and evidence. You may recognize these terms since TV cops and lawyers frequently use them. I want you to adapt what you think these terms mean related to criminal justice, and think of them in the context of writing an argument. **A claim is an idea to be proved. A reason is a more specific statement that supports a claim. And the evidence is textual proof from something you have read that supports the claim.**

The teacher goes on to provide examples and nonexamples of these three terms, coming back repeatedly to the student-friendly definitions and the examples and nonexamples. He then hands out graphic organizers and directs each of the previously organized student learning groups to skim through the unit on natural resources. He asks them to perform three tasks: identify a possible claim they could make as to how the availability of natural resources has influenced human activity; select at least one reason from science that might support the claim; and copy down one sentence from the text that supports the specific reason they have decided upon. While students are working in their groups, the teacher moves about, listening to their discussions for the critical content and reading the information they have written on their graphic organizers.

### Secondary Nonexample Using an Advance Organizer

The nonexample secondary teacher has the same goal for his students: to be able to write arguments focused on how the availability of natural resources has influenced human activity. His students have completed the same unit on natural resources, and he is prepared to identify the critical content students need to know.

> I've written three words on the board: *claim, reason, and evidence*. What do they communicate to you? *The students brainstorm situations related to criminal investigations.* I love legal thrillers and murder mysteries, but we're not going there in this class. We're going to look through our textbooks to find claims, reasons, and evidence for arguments related to natural resources. Pull out a piece of paper and write *claims, reasons,* and *evidence* at the top. Now look through this section on natural resources and identify claims, reasons, and evidence for how the availability of natural resources has influenced human activity.

The nonexample teacher's mistake was that he did not clearly define the critical content. Without this, students may not be able to interact with the critical content in this lesson. The teacher outlined a vague advance organizer that does not provide structure and support for students to stay focused on the critical content throughout the lesson. The purpose of an advance organizer is to help students identify what is critical and stay focused on it throughout the lesson. This nonexample does not help students do that.

## Determing If Students Can Identify Critical Content from Advance Organizers

You will only know that the advance organizer has achieved the desired result if your students are aware which content is important versus not important. To that end, two things have to happen:

1. Your students need to engage in some kind of action that requires them to demonstrate that they know the critical content in the advance organizer.

2. You, the teacher, must engage in some kind of monitoring action to listen, look for, read, check, inspect, or otherwise determine that your students do know what's important.

This two-step process ensures accountability. It lets you know whether your advance organizer helps your students focus on the critical content. Consider the following suggestions:

- As students are working on the advance organizer, read over their shoulders to ensure that they are identifying the critical content of the lesson.

- Ask your students to explain to a partner the important thing they want to remember from the advance organizer. Walk around listening to their conversations for critical information.

- Ask students to write a question to ask a partner about the critical content in the advance organizer. Circulate and listen as students discuss the answers. Then ask students to turn in those questions that they could not answer so you can answer them for the class.

- Ask students to highlight the critical content in the advance organizer. Walk around checking that students highlighted correct critical content.

Use the student proficiency scale for advance organizers to determine how well your students are progressing as you use various organizers to convey critical content to them.

**Student Proficiency Scale for Advance Organizers**

| Emerging | Fundamental | Desired Result |
|---|---|---|
| Students provide responses regarding the important information in the lesson. | Students provide accurate responses regarding the important information in the lesson. | Students provide comprehensive, accurate responses regarding the important information in the lesson. |
| Students can state some, but not all, of the important information in the lesson. | Students can explain which information is important in the lesson. | Students can explain why some information is important or not important in the lesson. |
| Students are able to restate critical information when called upon individually. | Students are able to respond with mostly correct critical information of the lesson when called upon individually. | Students are able to respond with the critical information of the lesson when called upon individually. |

# Scaffold and Extend Instruction to Meet Students' Needs

What do you do when you come up against the challenge of students who have already mastered the content or those who find the critical content too difficult to master at the same pace as other students? You adapt. That means you scaffold or extend the instruction to meet the needs of different groups of students.

## Scaffolding

Perhaps your struggling students could benefit from a reintroduction to the critical content using more explicit instruction. Or, they might benefit from an advance organizer that has more structure and guidance built in. You might give them sentence starters for completing an advance organizer or provide a list of key words that they will need to use.

## Extending

Perhaps you could ask your high-achieving students to adapt the advance organizer to tie in critical content from related lessons. You could push those advanced students to a higher level of thinking by asking them to develop a tool to target feedback on the critical content of the advance organizer. You also might think about allowing your students who have used advance organizers before to develop their own advance organizers conveying the critical content in a more unique way.

# Instructional Technique 5

# VISUALLY CUE CRITICAL CONTENT

Visual cueing is the use of one or more of the following visual media to convey critical content to students: video, demonstration, interactive website, storyboard, graphic organizer, illustration, photo, cartoon, work of art (such as a painting or sculpture), and illustrated PowerPoint slides. Other instructional techniques in this guide describe visual cueing used in tandem with other cueing techniques. For example, a teacher tells students what's important while pointing to a picture or drawing a chart on the board. Or, a teacher uses explicit instruction while illustrating a flowchart from which students can see the steps of solving a problem.

In this instructional technique, however, we focus on visual cueing as the *primary* way to convey critical content. Appealing to students' sense of sight is a powerful way to grab their attention and motivate them to connect with the content. A stunning video clip, a powerful photograph, or a superb graphic organizer has the potential to engage even the most reluctant students to tune in to critical content.

If you are an experienced educator, you know that some lessons are more difficult to teach than others. A visual cue may be just what is needed to make the lesson more memorable. When you and your students need a visual shot in the arm to cue the importance of new knowledge, select a cue that manages to motivate, engage, teach, and connect to prior learning in one perfect package.

## How to Effectively Implement Visual Cueing

The following is a list of things to keep in mind as you plan to implement visual cueing.

### Play to Your Strengths

Your strengths can guide you as you select the type of visual cue to use. If you love photography and have a collection of original photos, use them. You own the copyright to the photos, and they add a personal touch. If you specialize in fabulous PowerPoint presentations, develop a short one to cue the critical content. One way to increase your grade level's or department's library of visual cues is to team up with your colleagues and share productions.

### Avoid Controversial, Questionable, or Easily Misinterpreted Visual Cues

Take care to avoid anything that may be controversial or inappropriate. If in doubt, run your idea past your team leader, an administrator, or a colleague with a lot of experience. You simply want your students to know which content is important and unimportant.

### Make a Solid Connection

Do not lose sight of your purpose for selecting a visual cue—to aid students in the acquisition of new knowledge. Make sure you can articulate to yourself first and then to your students the reason you selected or created this particular visual cue. If the connection is too subtle or requires unrelated prior knowledge for comprehension, find another way to cue the critical content.

### Put Your Visual Cue to the Test

Show your visual cue to a colleague and ask him or her what critical content he or she thinks you are trying to convey. This should tell you if you hit the mark or not. If not, adapt the cue so that your students know exactly what the critical content is based on the visual cue.

## Common Mistakes

There are many ways a teacher might lose or confuse students when using visual cues to convey critical content:

- The teacher chooses a visual cue that is too difficult or broad for students to understand.

- The teacher selects a visual cue that fails to highlight the critical content he or she wants students to understand.

- The teacher fails to clearly explain how the visual cue relates to the critical content.

- The visual cue is too subtle for students to understand.

- The teacher employs a visual cue that requires prior knowledge that students do not have.

- The visual cue is so entertaining that students focus solely on its entertainment value and fail to identify and retain the critical content.

- The teacher selects a visual cue that may be interpreted as inappropriate or controversial.

- The teacher uses visual cueing excessively and students begin to tune it out.

## Visual Cueing in the Classroom

The visual cueing described here is more purposeful and complex than drawing a quick sketch on the board or pointing to a photo in the textbook. It takes preparation and an investment of time. Following are examples and nonexamples from elementary and secondary classrooms.

### Elementary Example of Visual Cueing

The elementary example illustrates how to use visual cueing when introducing critical content about reading comprehension. The standard is taken from the CCSS College and Career Readiness Anchor Standards for Reading Standard 1: *read closely to determine what the text says explicitly and to make logical inferences from it* (CCSS K–5 Reading). In the following example, the third grade teacher has prepared a poster to use as a visual cue during the lesson. She begins the lesson with the poster covered. The poster contains a cartoon drawing of a detective holding an oversized magnifying glass.

> I know you're eager to see what's on the easel. When I lift the black drape, I want complete silence. Then I'm going to choose someone to tell me the first thing you thought when you saw this poster. If someone gives the answer you were thinking, put your hand down. *The students suggest detectives, crimes, police, clues, and evidence.*

This year we are going to read like detectives. Every time we read, we are going to look for two kinds of clues. The first kind of clue shows us exactly what an author is telling us. Those clues are right there on the printed page. They are easier to find. We are also going to look for clues that aren't right there on the printed page. You will have to read like a detective and use your detective brain to find the hidden clues. Let me show you how this works. *The teacher writes a sentence on the board and models how she would first decide exactly what the author is telling the reader. Then she poses an inferential question for students that can be answered only from their prior knowledge and experiences. She thinks aloud for them about how she uses her detective brain to find hidden clues so she can answer the question.*

There are two important things you should look for when reading like a detective: clues that are right there on the printed page and ones that are hidden, which you will find in your detective brain.

*To practice this skill, the teacher passes out a set of statements with corresponding questions. The students will need to first look for the clues in the printed words, and then find the hidden ones in what they know and have experienced. The students work in pairs to complete the assignment as the teacher circulates the classroom, checking on their work.*

## Elementary Nonexample of Visual Cueing

In the nonexample elementary classroom, the teacher uses the detective motif on the worksheet she prepares for her students, suggesting that they might like to color the picture of the detective while she's explaining the worksheet to them. She does not talk about the significance of the detective, because she assumes her students will be able to make a connection between how detectives detect and how careful readers read. The teacher explains how to answer the questions on the worksheet without referring to the visual cue or linking reading to the detective graphic.

The mistake this teacher makes is that she does not link the critical content of the lesson to the visual cue. Without an overt linkage between those, many students do not make the connection between them. Therefore, the visual cue that she took time to locate and place on the worksheet was wasted.

### Secondary Example of Visual Cueing

In the secondary example the teacher wants students to understand how to view and interpret a political editorial cartoon as a way to analyze how historical contexts shaped and continue to shape perspectives.

Notice that we have two examples of cartoons on the front board. One is from the school newspaper, *Red Hawk News*, this week and one is from 1975. We're going to use these examples to learn how to "read" cartoons and to analyze how historical contexts shaped and continue to shape people's perspectives. Reading a cartoon is a bit different from reading a book or an article.

Let's concentrate on the recent cartoon to start. First, read the caption and see if you can identify what the cartoon is mainly about. You are well acquainted with the recent cartoon, but you might need a little more time to figure out the details of the cartoon from 1975.

Notice that this cartoon contains a caricature—an exaggerated and even humorous drawing of someone. In this cartoon, the caricature represents our basketball coach. We know that Mr. Loveland's ears don't stick out quite that much and his beard isn't quite that scraggly. That is sometimes an important part of a political cartoon—a caricature of an individual who is involved in the event. Also notice that this cartoon contains a symbol, an object that stands for an idea. In our cartoon, the profile of an American Indian is a symbol of Chief Red Hawk, the controversial individual for whom our teams are named. Later in the lesson, we will look at how this symbol has changed from 1975 to now.

The last thing to consider when you're "reading" a political cartoon is the opinion or message the cartoonist is trying to convey and whether he or she seems to have any particular bias. We'll spend some time talking about this in order to analyze how historical contexts shaped and continue to shape people's perspectives related to these cartoons.

*The teacher points to various parts of the cartoon as she reminds students how to read a cartoon.* Let's review what's important about reading a political cartoon: 1) read the caption and identify what the cartoon is mainly about; 2) identify any caricatures that help you figure out the meaning of the cartoon; 3) look for symbols that may stand for a certain idea or perspective; and 4) figure out the opinion or message the cartoonist is trying to convey.

To represent students' knowledge and monitor whether students know what is important about reading a political cartoon, the teacher passes out a brief organizer on which students can write their responses regarding the four items they will "read" from the second cartoon. Once students begin working, the teacher walks around ensuring that students are able to complete the organizer with the critical content from the cartoon.

### Secondary Nonexample of Visual Cueing
Now let's go into this same lesson presented by a teacher down the hall.

Let's talk about what's important about reading a political cartoon to analyze how historical contexts shaped and continue to shape people's perspectives. Who can tell me what you think is necessary to notice when reading a political cartoon? *Students respond with many answers, including the four statements the teacher was hoping to hear:*

*1) read the caption and identify what the cartoon is mainly about; 2) identify any caricatures that help you figure out the meaning of the cartoon; 3) look for symbols that may stand for a certain idea or perspective; and 4) figure out the opinion or message the cartoonist is trying to convey.*

Those are all good answers. Now that we've talked about how to read a political cartoon, try it yourself. Here is a cartoon from a recent edition of our school newspaper. Use this organizer to answer questions about this cartoon. *The teacher then passes out the organizer and students begin to work.*

Notice that this teacher is using the same resources as the previous teacher. Sometimes, mistakes occur not because of the resources you use but how you use them. This teacher made the common mistake of failing to clearly explain how the visual cue relates to the critical content. She did not give students the opportunity to understand the essential steps of reading a political cartoon.

## Determining If Students Can Identify Critical Content from Visual Cueing

The only way to determine if your visual cueing is successful is to have students identify the critical content. Plan in advance the tasks you will ask students to do. Both of the example teachers had an idea and materials prepared to accomplish that task during the time limits of the class period. They allocated time to walk around, listen, and check to see that students were connecting what they learned from the visual cue to their learning target. Here is a list of ways that you can monitor whether your students are able to identify critical content as a result of visual cueing:

- Students display nonverbal signals such as thumbs up–thumbs down or arms crossed–arms uncrossed to indicate their choice of important or unimportant information. The teacher scans the classroom to note whether students have made the correct choice.

- Students fold a piece of plain paper into fourths, using each of the sections to write responses related to the critical content, and then hold them up for the teacher to read as he or she circulates the classroom.

- Students pair with a numbered partner and explain the critical content to each other while the teacher circulates and listens. Students can be permanently numbered one or two, and the teacher gives a direction such as, "Ones tell the twos a piece of important information you learned from this picture."

- Students place a sticky arrow or flag on the part of the visual that is critical content. The teacher looks through the flags for accurate critical content.

The student proficiency scale for visual cueing will help you assess how well your students are progressing in identifying critical content from the visual cues you employ in a lesson. Use this scale to help you monitor for the desired result of visual cueing.

**Student Proficiency Scale for Visually Cueing Content**

| Emerging | Fundamental | Desired Result |
|----------|-------------|----------------|
| Students identify information in the visual cue. | Students can list the critical content in the visual cue. | Students can explain how the visual cue represents the critical content of the lesson. |
| Students explain how the visual cue relates to the lesson. | Students can explain how the visual cue relates to the learning target. | Students are able to explain how the visual cue relates to the sequence of the critical content to reach the learning target. |

# Scaffold and Extend Instruction to Meet Students' Needs

The ways in which you scaffold or extend visual cueing depend on which type of visual cue you have selected. With multiple types of visual cues to choose from, you can readily meet the needs of students who need additional instructional support or motivation to extend their learning to a more challenging level.

## Scaffolding

Consider how the elementary teacher in the example might have provided scaffolding for students who had a difficult time reading the sentence and finding clues to answer the question. She could have provided students with a set of answers and asked them to match these answers to the appropriate question. The high school teacher who discovered that students were having a difficult time finding the appropriate parts of the political cartoon could provide a version that has these parts numbered to correspond with the questions. Other ways you might provide support for students for visual cues include highlighting the parts of the cue you want students to focus on or providing key words for students to use to describe the visual cue.

## Extending

Often you will have students capable of creating or finding their own visual cues. If that is the case, give those students guidelines so they stay focused on the critical content. Another way to extend is to ask them to brainstorm how they can improve the visual cue to be more helpful with identifying critical content. You can also ask students to create a key for complicated visual cues that could help other students decipher the meaning of it.

## Instructional Technique 6

# USE STORYTELLING TO CUE CRITICAL CONTENT

Storytelling is a powerful way to identify critical content. It is a technique that famous orators of the past and popular speakers of the present have honed to perfection. Stories can be compelling and even entertaining, but *your* purpose in telling a story is to give students a way to understand and remember critical content. Whether the stories are from something you read about or your own life experiences, you must select them solely for their power in making critical content more memorable for your students. As with other instructional techniques, storytelling does not guarantee an effective lesson.

## How to Effectively Implement Storytelling

Storytelling is a powerful way to convey critical content about global concepts. Effective storytelling is a specialized version of dramatic instruction. If you love to read aloud to students and frequently show pictures and "tell" the story, you might already be an accomplished storyteller. A well-told story holds the power to draw even the most reluctant students into the content. So, if you have a group of resistant learners, look for a story to tell. You may have them in the palm of your hand right from the start. Consider using stories from history, literature, sports, science, entertainment, or your own personal experience. Here are some ways to effectively implement storytelling.

### Connect the Story to Critical Content

Think of storytelling as a way to reach students who may be more creative and aren't always engaged in direct instruction. It shows students what you want them to do, or think, in a more indirect fashion. As you choose a story for a particular lesson, make sure there is a clear connection between the story and the critical content. Also, be confident that you are able to explain this connection to students at the close of the story or lesson.

### Rehearse, Rehearse, Rehearse

There's no substitute for telling your story several times to polish the rough edges. Remember, you are "telling" the story. Telling requires maintaining eye contact with your students and reading their body language. Story-telling requires expression and even some body and hand movements. Storytelling often improves with a slightly slower speed of talking and can also pack more punch with a dramatic moment of silence here and there as appropriate.

### Keep It Short and Simple

Keep the story you tell simple and short. Your story should take no more than three to four minutes. Avoid jargon and too many big words. Your students need to be able to process your story and build mental images as you relate it.

### Use Stories Judiciously

It's important to remember that the purpose of storytelling is to identify critical content. Ensure that you're not sacrificing instruction time with your storytelling, you're enhancing it. If the majority of your lesson is sto-rytelling, when would students have an opportunity to process and deepen their understanding?

### Begin with the End in Mind

Your goal in using a story to cue critical information is to increase the likeli-hood that your students will know what content is important and what is not. So, as you begin to tell your story, keep in mind that your goal is not to enter-tain so much as to make the lesson content memorable for your students.

## Common Mistakes

There are a few mistakes that can occur in the course of using storytelling to cue critical content:

- The story does not highlight the critical content.

- The teacher does not explain how the story ties to the critical content of the lesson.

- The story is too long or complex for students to understand.

- The story does not interest students.

## Storytelling in the Classroom

Both elementary and secondary examples and nonexamples are based on Standard 10 of the College and Career Readiness Anchor Standards for Reading: *read and comprehend complex literary and informational texts independently and proficiently.*

### Elementary Example of Storytelling

The elementary example using storytelling to cue critical content comes from a fourth grade teacher who was an English language learner (ELL) in early elementary school. Here is the story she tells her students.

> We have a big goal to meet this year: reading more books, reading harder books, and learning new things from these books. I came to the United States when I was seven years old. I was in second grade and I was scared. I didn't understand English and I didn't know how to read. I bet you are wondering, "How did you get to be so smart that you could be a teacher?" Two things helped me: 1) I came to school every day, paid attention, and did my homework, and 2) I started to read. In the beginning, I could read only easy books, but that didn't matter. I just kept reading more, and pretty soon I was reading harder ones. I read all the time. I read before school in the morning, during lunchtime, and sometimes I even read books after I was supposed to go to sleep at night. I read stories, but I also read books about space, animals, and famous people. When I didn't know what a word meant, I asked somebody or looked it up.
>
> This year, our class is going to read many books, and by the end of the year, the books will be harder than the books we start with. How will we do that? We are going to come to school every day, pay attention, and do our homework, and we are going to become reading machines that just don't quit. If I can do what I did when I was in second grade, you can do the very same thing.

This story highlights the importance of reading and helps students see that reading with increasing complexity takes practice. This teacher kept the story short and focused on the critical content of how to increase proficiency by reading varied texts and learning new words.

### Elementary Nonexample of Storytelling

The elementary nonexample begins in a similar fashion.

> We have a big goal to meet this year: reading more books, reading harder books, and learning new things from these books. I came to the United States when I was seven years old. I was in second grade and I was scared. I didn't understand English and I didn't know how to read. If I can learn to read, so can you. This year, our class is going to read many books, and by the end of the year, the books will be harder than the books we start with. *The teacher then begins to read the book she selected.*

This teacher misses the mark because her story is so brief that it doesn't address the critical content of increasing proficiency by reading varied texts and learning new words. Students may not even realize that the intention of the story was to identify critical content. They may think the teacher just wanted to tell them a little about herself.

### Secondary Example of Storytelling

In the secondary example of using storytelling to identify critical content, we're listening in on an interventionist who supports ELLs and other struggling students.

> I want to tell you a story about how reading changed my life. When I was young, I didn't like to read that much. I didn't find books I liked until I was a sophomore in high school. Some of

you may be like I was then. Somehow that year, I encountered two books that really got me into reading in such a way that I couldn't stop. I guess I would have never considered going to college or becoming a teacher if I hadn't discovered how wonderful reading was. My first book was **The Godfather**. *Some of the students are laughing at the title.* I know you're finding it hard to believe that your sweet, gentle teacher could get turned on to reading by such a gory book. But it grabbed me. The second book that really got my attention was **Gone with the Wind**. It was filled with Civil War history and romance. Neither of these books will be on your reading list this year. But that's OK. Sometimes you just need to find a book that you want to read. Don't stop trying to find that one. It will change your life when you do.

This story illustrates to students the need to find stories that interest them in wanting to practice reading to increase proficiency. The teacher gave a couple examples, and then tied the story together at the end by referring back to the critical content of increasing proficiency by finding stories that interest them.

### Secondary Nonexample of Storytelling

The secondary nonexample of storytelling features the same teacher telling the story slightly differently.

I want to tell you a story about how reading changed my life. When I was young, I didn't like to read that much. I didn't find books I liked until I was a sophomore in high school. Some of you may be like I was then. Somehow that year, I encountered a book that really got me into reading in such a way that I couldn't stop. I guess I would have never considered going to college or becoming a teacher if I hadn't discovered how wonderful reading was. My first book was **The Godfather**. Some *of the students are laughing at the title.* I know you're finding it hard to believe that your sweet, gentle teacher could get turned on to reading by such a gory book. But it grabbed me. *The teacher then describes in detail the plot of **The Godfather**, which takes ten minutes of class time because of all the questions the students ask. The teacher ends the story with:* This book will not be on your reading list this year. But that's OK. Sometimes you just need to find a book that you want to read. Don't stop trying to find that one. It will change your life when you do.

The teacher in this nonexample is sharing her love of reading, but makes the mistake of telling a story that is too long for students to stay focused on the critical content. Although this version of the story contains the same critical content as the first, many students may miss it since it was not the central focus of this story. The plot of *The Godfather* was.

## Determining If Students Can Identify Critical Content from Storytelling

The following suggestions can help you know if students can identify critical content from storytelling:

- Ask students to draw a picture illustrating some aspect of the critical content. Walk around and discuss the illustrations as your students draw.

- Place students into learning groups to discuss the main ideas of the story. Walk around and listen to make sure students are able to identify critical content of the story.

- Have students sort pictures that relate to the story into two categories: things that are important to do and things that are not important.

Use the student proficiency scale for storytelling to check that you are achieving the desired result with storytelling.

**Student Proficiency Scale for Storytelling to Cue Critical Content**

| Emerging | Fundamental | Desired Result |
|---|---|---|
| Students listen to the story. | Students can retell critical parts of the story. | Students can summarize the story using critical content. |
| Students can retell parts of the story. | Students can list the critical content contained in the story. | Students are able to describe the critical content contained in the story. |
| Students can identify some critical content of the lesson that relates to the story. | Students can describe some linkages between the story and the critical content of the lesson. | Students can explain how the story illustrates the critical content of the lesson. |

# Scaffold and Extend Instruction to Meet Students' Needs

When you plan ahead for scaffolding and extending instruction, you are more likely to adapt to students' needs during the lesson. There is no need to create elaborate support tools or large extension projects. Think about what small things you can do to help students grow from wherever they are.

## Scaffolding

- Develop private signals with students to refocus their attention on critical content during the story (for example, touch your chin, make a hand symbol, or point to a visual cue).

- Provide a written copy of the story with the critical content highlighted.

- Prepare a list of questions to hand to students who are unable to identify critical content in a story without support.

## Extending

- Have students create their own stories that illustrate the critical content of the lesson.

- Ask students to identify which parts of the story were more critical than others.

## Instructional Technique 7

# USE WHAT STUDENTS ALREADY KNOW TO CUE CRITICAL CONTENT

Students come into your class with prior knowledge—sometimes more than you think and sometimes less than you hope for. No matter how much or how little, though, you can leverage what students already know to help cue critical content of the lesson. The practice of activating prior knowledge is based on research showing how skilled readers process content in their specific disciplines. Skilled readers reflected aloud for researchers about what they were thinking while reading. A consensus emerged around the frequency with which the readers made connections from their prior learning and experiences to new concepts and helped them generate new hypotheses (Pressley & Afflerbach, 1995).

To use what students already know to cue critical content, plan ahead for what you think they should know as well as how to determine whether they do know it.

## How to Effectively Implement Using What Students Already Know to Cue Critical Content

### Make Sure Students Understand Crucial Vocabulary and Basic Facts

If you have been teaching the same content or grade level for any length of time, you may be able to predict the common knowledge gaps and strengths your students may have regarding crucial vocabulary and basic facts. However, just when you think you've heard it all, a student may pop up with a misunderstanding you weren't expecting. As you introduce content, check that students understand crucial vocabulary and basic facts. If they don't, provide a brief explanation or illustration that you have prepared in advance.

### Make Sure Students Understand Basic Relationships

When you cue critical content, you must be able to understand and signal to your students the relationship between concepts. Use the learning target of the day as a springboard for your thought process about this step. What is the relationship between the concepts within the learning target, and how can you convey this to your students? There are four types of relationships to consider:

- One thing is a cause or consequence of the other.

- As one thing gets larger, the other systematically gets smaller or larger.

- The two things are similar or dissimilar to each other in specific ways.

- One thing is an example or type of the other.

### Make Sure Students Possess Basic Skills and Processes

Students sometimes become masters at covering up when they don't possess basic skills and processes. Determine the prerequisite skills and processes a student needs to know to learn the skill or process you are teaching. Prepare to check that students have those basic skills, or adapt your lesson if they don't.

### Make Sure Students Possess Illustrative Mental Models

Many concepts that you will teach are intangible, such as time in first grade or subatomic particles in high school. For students to grasp these concepts, they must have mental models of them. A mental model is an image you think of that represents information or a process. Think carefully about the concept you want to teach so that you can describe your mental model of it to your students. Be purposeful in class to help your students formulate their own mental models about critical content. Illustrations and simulations can be helpful for teaching mental models.

## Common Mistakes

As with the other techniques, there are some common mistakes that teachers need to avoid when using what students already know to cue critical content:

- The teacher fails to make sure that students understand crucial vocabulary and facts.

- The teacher misidentifies the relationship between concepts.

- The teacher assumes students are competent in prerequisite skills.

- The teacher does not allow time for students to formulate their own mental models.

- The teacher fails to summarize and assess what students actually learned.

## Examples and Nonexamples of Using What Students Already Know to Cue Critical Content

Following are two sets of examples and nonexamples, one from elementary classrooms and another from secondary classrooms.

### Elementary Example of Using What Students Already Know

The elementary example of using what students already know to cue critical content is based on a first grade science standard: *use observation of the sun, moon, and stars to describe patterns that can be predicted* (Next Generation Science Standards, 2013). The teacher has prepared four cards for each set of partners. Each card depicts the sun in different stages: rising, setting, high in the sky, and one card dark with no sun at all.

Today, we're going to talk about patterns in the sky. Some people use telescopes to observe things in the sky. We are going to find out how much we know about space from looking at it with our own eyes. The objects in the sky we are going to talk about are predictable. That means we can depend on these objects to be in certain places in the sky at certain times. I want to remind you before we begin that there are certain objects we might see in the sky that don't count: birds, planes, balloons, or helicopters. These things come and go; they do not have predictable patterns. Now, who can tell us something you have observed about the sun that is predictable?

*One student ventures that he's seen the sun coming up in the morning. The teacher commends his powers of observation and elaborates on his description to explain that scientists have a special word for the sun "coming up."* We say the sun is rising, and the exact moment that we can see the sun rising is called *sunrise.* Do you know that word? Say it to your partner. Find the picture card that matches that word.

*The teacher then asks for more observations and sees another student with her hand raised.* You look as though you might have observed something else about the sun. Tell us. *The student explains that the sun doesn't just rise, it sets. She goes on to say that she sees this at night before she goes to bed.* The word for that is *sunset.* Say that word to your partner, and find the picture card that matches that word. *The teacher pauses for students to do that, watching partners to see if they pick the correct card.*

We now have two observations about the sun: it rises and it sets. What else have you observed about the sun? Is there a predictable pattern? Tell your partner. *The teacher allows time for the students to discuss where they've seen the sun at different times of the day.* What is the predictable pattern of the sun in the sky each day? Order your cards to show the predictable pattern of the sun in the sky. *The teacher walks around guiding and encouraging students as needed.*

In this example, the teacher uses the cards to help students create a mental model of the pattern of the sun in the sky. She first makes sure students know the crucial vocabulary. Then she guides them to think about the relationship of their observations of the sun.

### Elementary Nonexample of Using What Students Already Know

The nonexample lesson starts the same way but lacks the necessary actions of using what students already know to cue critical content. This teacher is addressing the same standard but does not have the sets of sun cards.

Today, we're going to talk about patterns in the sky. Some people use telescopes to observe things in the sky. We are going to find out how much we know about space from looking at it with our own eyes. The objects in the sky we are going to talk about are predictable. That means we can depend on these objects to be in certain places in the sky at certain times. I want to remind you before we begin that there are certain objects we might see in the sky that don't count: birds, planes, balloons, or helicopters. These things come and go; they do not have predictable patterns. Now, who can tell us something you have observed about the sun that is predictable? *One student ventures that he's seen the sun coming up in the morning. The teacher commends his powers of observation and elaborates on his description to explain that scientists have a special word for the sun "coming up."* We say the sun is rising, and the exact moment that we can see the sun rising is called *sunrise. The teacher then asks for more observations and sees another student with her hand raised.* You look as though you might have observed something else about the sun. Tell us. *The student explains that the sun doesn't just rise, it sets. She goes on to say that she sees this at night before she goes to bed.* The word for that is *sunset.* We now have two observations about the sun: it rises and it sets. What is the predictable pattern of the sun in the sky each day? *The teacher listens as a third student describes sunrise and sunset. Then she asks the other students to tell their partners what they know about sunrise and sunset.*

The nonexample teacher simply asks a few students to share their observations, instead of making sure students understand crucial vocabulary and basic facts or helping them formulate a mental model. The teacher is not aware, from this activity, which students know the key words or are able to use observations to describe the predictable pattern of the sun in the sky.

*Secondary Example of Using What Students Already Know*

The secondary example is based on the following learning target: *develop and use a model of the earth-sun system to describe the cyclic patterns of seasons.*

Today, we're going to discuss what we know about the seasons of the year. As you tell me what you know, I'm going to write it down on the board. When we finish writing down what we know, we will then figure out if what we believe about the seasons matches the correct scientific knowledge.

*As her students share what they believe, the teacher develops the following list:*

- We have seasons because of how far away the earth is from the sun. In the summer we're close to the sun and in the winter we're far away from the sun.

- I know the earth tilts, and I think it tilts closer to the sun in the summer and far away from the sun in the winter.

- The earth is constantly moving and that causes day and night. In the summer there are longer days and in the winter the days are shorter.

*The teacher quickly realizes that her students have several misconceptions about the critical content of this learning target. The teacher then has the students in small groups develop and use a model to describe the cyclic patterns of seasons. She tells the students that the model needs to demonstrate the earth's rotation on its axis as well as the planet's orbit around the sun. She helps students focus on which hemisphere gets more direct light at different positions of the earth's orbit. Students will then decide whether the statements on the board are true or false and explain why using the model.*

This example targets two actions. After determining that students in the class were unable to identify the relationship between critical content (seasons and the hemispheres receiving direct and indirect solar energy), the teacher had an activity ready to help students develop a mental model for this critical content. By having the students develop the model themselves, the teacher allows students to form their own mental images from the experience of using the physical model.

*Secondary Nonexample of Using What Students Already Know*

The secondary nonexample teacher believes that if students have misconceptions, they shouldn't be discussed in class. The other students might get confused by incorrect answers mentioned in class. She instead starts the class by having students read a short piece of text that explains rotation and orbit. Then she asks two students to come to the front and act as the sun and the earth as she talks through the cause for seasons.

In both of these activities in the nonexample, the students are passive learners. Neither activity requires that students demonstrate they know what content is critical. The teacher does not check that students understand the relationship between the critical content, nor does she ensure that students have developed their own mental models for the cause of seasons.

## Determining If Students Can Use What They Already Know to Identify Critical Content

When the content is critical and you want to use what students already know to cue it, you must monitor throughout. What questions can you ask? How can you get your students, not just one or two of them, to respond during each of the four actions of using what students already know to cue critical content? While they are responding, how can you see or hear evidence that they understand crucial vocabulary and basic facts, understand basic relationships, possess basic skills and processes, and possess illustrative mental models? Try these suggestions for monitoring whether students can use what they already know to cue critical content:

- Students explain to a partner as you walk around and listen.

- Students sort vocabulary cards as you check to ensure that they have a working knowledge of key words.

- Students represent their mental models and you examine the representations.

- Students list the steps to the basic skills and processes, and you check them for accuracy.

Use the student proficiency scale to assess your students' progress toward proficiency in lessons where you use what students already know to cue critical content.

**Student Proficiency Scale for Using What Students Already Know to Cue Critical Content**

| Emerging | Fundamental | Desired Result |
|---|---|---|
| Students are familiar with the vocabulary and basic facts. | Students understand crucial vocabulary and basic facts. | Students can use and apply crucial vocabulary and basic facts. |
| Students can identify basic relationships between critical content. | Students understand basic relationships between critical content. | Students are able to explain basic relationships between critical content. |
| Students are familiar with basic skills and processes. | Students possess basic skills and processes. | Students are able to apply basic skills and processes. |
| Students can imagine the mental model as explained by the teacher. | Students possess illustrative mental models. | Students use mental models to understand and apply the critical content. |

# Scaffold and Extend Instruction to Meet Students' Needs

Scaffolding and extending for your students can provide mutually beneficial experiences for struggling students who need repeated exposures to the critical content and students who have knowledge to share with their classmates.

## Scaffolding

- Provide students with a graphic organizer that has completed examples of crucial vocabulary and basic facts that connect to the critical content.

- Ask students to think aloud when talking about relationships to discover the source of their errors or confusion.

- Use pictures or physical models to enhance the spoken or written explanations of mental models.

## Extending

- Students create their own personal organizer that shows connections between critical content.

- Students can work together to create questions about crucial vocabulary, facts, skills, and processes.

- Students can nonlinguistically represent their mental models in various ways.

# Conclusion

The goal of this guide is to enable you to become more effective in teaching content to your students. The beginning step, as you learned in the preceding pages, is to become skilled at helping students identify critical content. To determine if this goal has been met, you will need to gather information from your students and engage in a meaningful self-reflection. If you acquire nothing else from this guide, let it be the *importance of monitoring*. The tipping point in your expertise and student achievement is *monitoring*; it isn't enough to simply implement the strategy.

To be the most effective you can be, view implementation as a three-step process. First implement the strategy. In this case, identify critical content in the lesson in such a way that students know what is important and what is not. Next, monitor for the desired result. In other words, while you are implementing the strategy, determine whether that strategy is effective with your students. For the *identifying critical content* strategy, check in real time to immediately see or hear whether students know if certain content is critical or not. Finally, as a result of your monitoring, if you realize that the way in which you cued the critical content was not effective with all students, adapt your approach by supporting or extending your instruction so that *all* students know what is important about the lesson. This puts monitoring at the heart of implementation, which is where it should be in effective instruction.

Although you can experience this guide and gain expertise independently, the process will be more beneficial if you read and work through the content with colleagues.

## Reflection and Discussion Questions

Use the following reflection and discussion questions during a team meeting or even as food for thought prior to a meeting with your coach, mentor, or supervisor:

1. How has your instruction changed as a result of reading and implementing the instructional techniques found in this guide?

2.  What ways have you found to modify and enhance the instructional techniques found in this guide to scaffold and enhance your instruction?

3.  What was your biggest challenge in implementing the instructional strategy featured in this guide?

4.  How would you describe the changes in your students' learning that have occurred as a result of implementing this instructional strategy?

5.  What will you do to share what you have learned with colleagues at your grade level or in your department?

# References

Ausubel, D. (1960). The use of advance organizers in the learning and retention of meaningful verbal material. *Journal of Educational Psychology, 51,* 267–272.

Ausubel, E., Novak, J., & Hanesian, H. (1978). *Educational psychology: A cognitive view* (2nd ed.). New York, NY: Holt, Rinehart & Winston.

Common Core State Standards Initiative. (2010). *Common Core State Standards for English language arts & literacy in history/social studies, science, and technical subjects.* Washington, DC: Author. Retrieved September 23, 2011, from http://corestandards.org/assets/CCSSI_ELA%20Standards.pdf

Dickson, S. V., Collins, V. L., Simmons, D. C., & Kame'enui, E. J. (1998). Metacognitive strategies: Instructional and curricular basics and implications. In D. C. Simmons & E. J. Kame'enui (Eds.), *What reading research tells us about children with diverse learning needs* (pp. 361–380). Hillsdale, NJ: Erlbaum.

Keene, E. O., & Zimmerman, S. (1997). *Mosaic of thought: Teaching comprehension in a reader's workshop.* Portsmouth, NH: Heinemann.

Marzano, R. J. (2013, November). Art and science of teaching: Planning for what students don't know. *Educational Leadership, 71*(3), 80–81..

Marzano, R. J., Boogren, T., Heflebower, T., Kanold-McIntyre, J., & Pickering, D. (2012). *Becoming a reflective teacher.* Bloomington, IN: Marzano Research Laboratory.

Marzano, R. J., & Brown, J. L. (2009). *A handbook for the art and science of teaching.* Alexandria, VA: Association for Supervision and Curriculum Development.

Marzano, R. J. (2007). *The art and science of teaching.* Alexandria, VA: Association for Supervision and Curriculum Development.

Marzano, R. J., & Toth, M. D. (2013). *Deliberate practice for deliberate growth: Teacher evaluation systems for continuous instructional improvement.* West Palm Beach, FL: Learning Sciences Marzano Center.

National Governors Association Center for Best Practices, Council of Chief State School Officers. (2010). *Common Core State Standards.* Washington, DC: Author.

NGSS Lead States. (2013). *Next generation science standards: For states, by states.* Washington, DC: National Academies Press. Retrieved October 11, 2013, from http://www.nextgenscience.org/next-generation-science-standards

Ogle, D. M. (1986). K-W-L: A teaching model that develops active reading of expository text. *The Reading Teacher, 26,* 564–570.

Pressley, M., & Afflerbach, P. (1995). *Verbal protocols of reading: The nature of constructively responsive reading.* Hillsdale, NJ: Erlbaum.

Schank, R. (1999). *Dynamic memory revisited.* Cambridge, UK: Cambridge University Press.

# Index

## A

advance organizers
    common mistakes, 39–40
    defined, 37
    examples and nonexamples, 40–43
    extending instruction, 45
    implementing, 38–39
    metaphors, use of, 38
    monitoring for desired result, 43–44
    scaffolding, 45
    student proficiency scale for, 44
Ausubel, D., 37

## C

CCR (College and Career Readiness)
    Anchor Standards, defined, 2
CCSS (Common Core State Standards),
    defined, 2
CCSSI (Common Core State Standards
    Initiative), 2
College and Career Readiness. *See* CCR
Common Core State Standards. *See*
    CCSS
Common Core State Standards Initiative.
    *See* CCSSI
content, 2

## D

desired result
    defined, 2
    monitoring for the, 8–9
dramatic instruction
    common mistakes, 30–31
    examples and nonexamples, 31–33
    extending instruction, 35
    implementing, 29–30
    monitoring for desired result,
    33–34
    scaffolding, 35
    student proficiency scale for, 34

## E

explicit instruction
    chunking critical content, 22
    common mistakes, 23
    examples and nonexamples,
    23–26
    extending instruction, 28
    identifying critical content, 21
    implementing, 21–22
    modeling critical content, 21–22
    monitoring for desired result,
    26–27
    scaffolding, 28
    student-friendly definitions, use
    of, 22
    student proficiency scale for, 27
extending
    defined, 2
    instruction to meet students'
    needs, 9–10

## I

identifying critical content strategy
    behaviors associated with, 7
    common mistakes, 7–8
    failing to communicate the
    importance of, 7–8

# Notes

# Notes

# Notes

# Notes